James Madison

Pamela McDowell

LET'S READ AV² BY WEIGL™
ADDED VALUE • AUDIO VISUAL

Go to **www.av2books.com**, and enter this book's unique code.

BOOK CODE

K 9 5 4 3 3 8

AV² by Weigl brings you media enhanced books that support active learning.

AV² provides enriched content that supplements and complements this book. Weigl's AV² books strive to create inspired learning and engage young minds in a total learning experience.

Your AV² Media Enhanced books come alive with...

Audio
Listen to sections of the book read aloud.

Video
Watch informative video clips.

Embedded Weblinks
Gain additional information for research.

Try This!
Complete activities and hands-on experiments.

Key Words
Study vocabulary, and complete a matching word activity.

Quizzes
Test your knowledge.

Slide Show
View images and captions, and prepare a presentation.

... and much, much more!

Published by AV² by Weigl
350 5th Avenue, 59th Floor New York, NY 10118
Websites: www.av2books.com www.weigl.com

Library of Congress Control Number: 2014934872

ISBN 978-1-4896-1058-4 (hardcover)
ISBN 978-1-4896-1059-1 (softcover)
ISBN 978-1-4896-1060-7 (single user eBook)
ISBN 978-1-4896-1061-4 (multi-user eBook)

Printed in the United States of America in North Mankato, Minnesota
1 2 3 4 5 6 7 8 9 0 18 17 16 15 14

052014
WEP150314

Project Coordinator: Jared Siemens
Designer: Ana María Vidal

Every reasonable effort has been made to trace ownership and to obtain permission to reprint copyright material. The publishers would be pleased to have any errors or omissions brought to their attention so that they may be corrected in subsequent printings.

Weigl acknowledges Getty Images as the primary image supplier for this title.

CONTENTS

Who Is James Madison?

James Madison was one of the Founding Fathers of the United States. He is known as the "Father of the Constitution." This is because he wrote the main laws of the United States. Madison used his skills as a thinker and writer to fight for America's freedom from British rule. He was the fourth president of the United States.

What Is a Founding Father?

As a Founding Father, James Madison fought to free the American colonies from the rule of Great Britain. This freedom led the colonies to form a new country. This country was the United States of America. Madison wrote the most important laws of the country. These laws are called the U.S. Constitution. The Constitution says how the people are to be ruled.

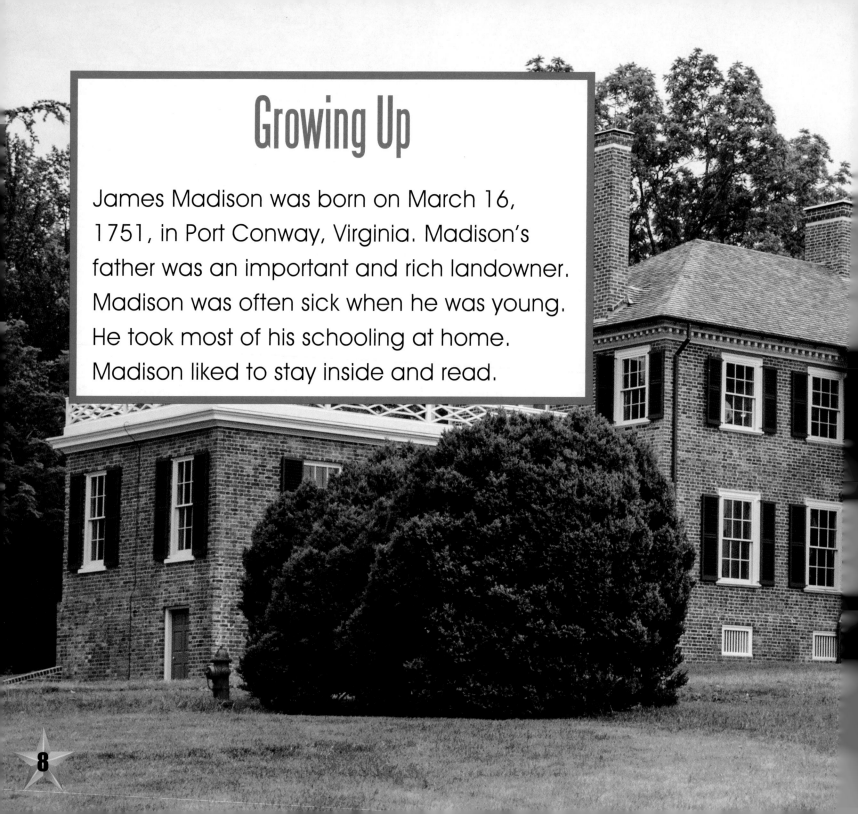

Growing Up

James Madison was born on March 16, 1751, in Port Conway, Virginia. Madison's father was an important and rich landowner. Madison was often sick when he was young. He took most of his schooling at home. Madison liked to stay inside and read.

Learning From Others

James Madison read many books. He learned new ideas from the books he read. Madison felt he owed everything to one of his teachers. This teacher taught Madison about important thinkers and writers of his day. Madison soon became a great thinker and writer as well.

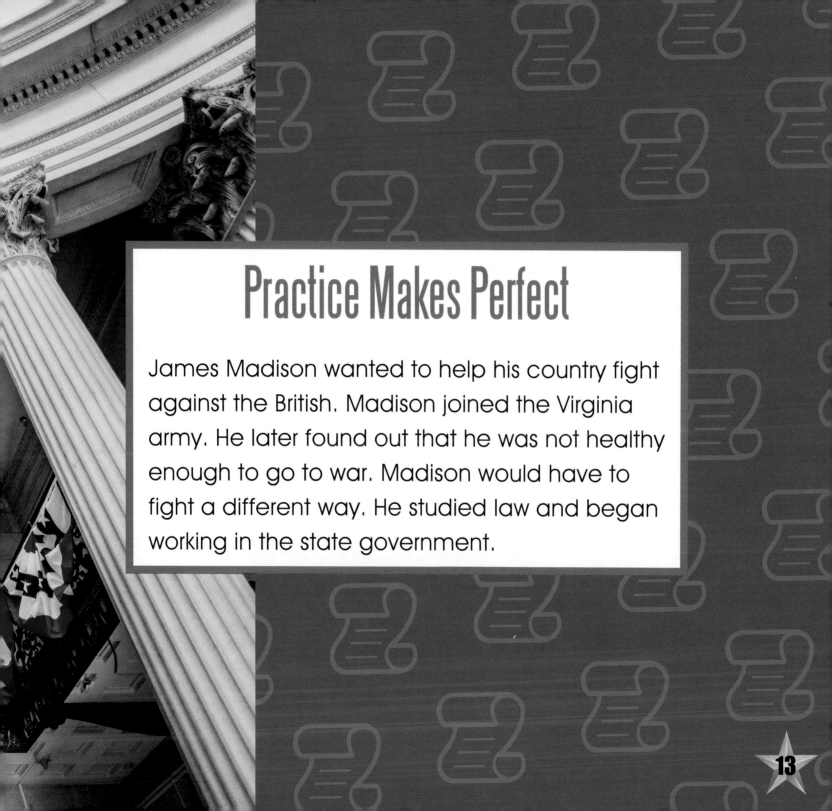

Practice Makes Perfect

James Madison wanted to help his country fight against the British. Madison joined the Virginia army. He later found out that he was not healthy enough to go to war. Madison would have to fight a different way. He studied law and began working in the state government.

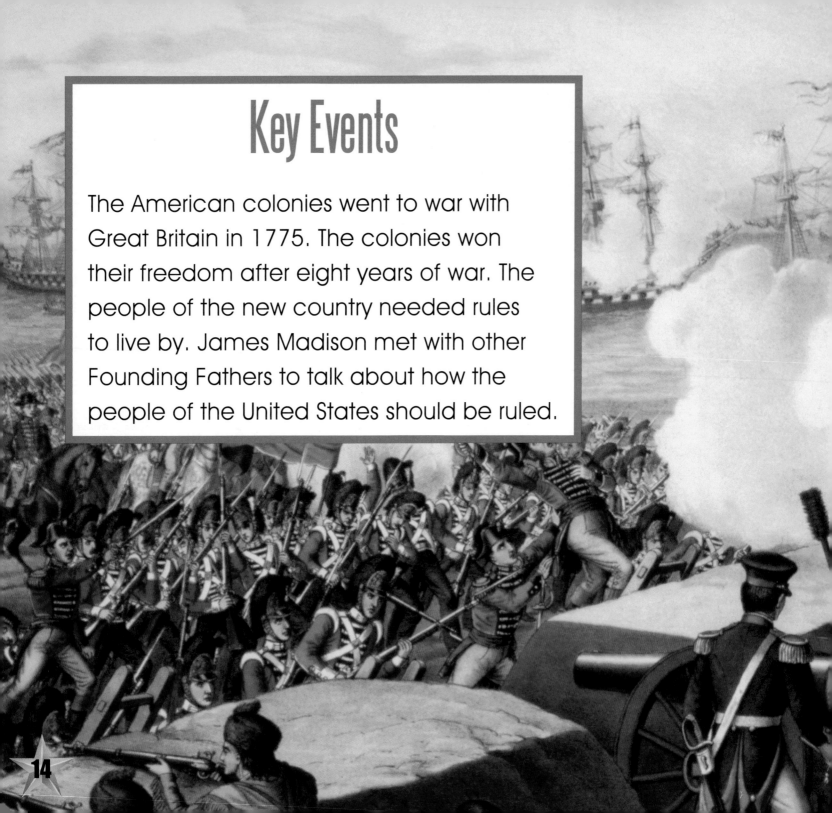

Key Events

The American colonies went to war with Great Britain in 1775. The colonies won their freedom after eight years of war. The people of the new country needed rules to live by. James Madison met with other Founding Fathers to talk about how the people of the United States should be ruled.

Challenges

James Madison had many ideas about how the new country should work. He wanted the country to be ruled fairly. Madison thought power should not rest in the hands of one person or group. He thought power should be shared. Madison wrote these ideas into the Constitution of the United States of America.

A Nation Is Born

James Madison wanted to make sure the American people had rights. Rights are laws that keep people safe. He wrote these rights into the Constitution. Madison wrote most of the Constitution. He was elected president in 1809. Madison was president for eight years.

Article III.

...United States, shall be vested in one supreme Court... both of the supreme and inferior Courts, sha... which shall not be diminished during their... extend to all Cases, in Law and Equity, arising... thority;— to all Cases affecting Ambassadors... cies to which the United States shall be a ... zens of different States,— between Citizens... and foreign States, Citizens or Subjects... bassadors, other public Ministers and Co... for Cases before mentioned, the supreme... as the Congress shall make...

... the Service of the United ... employed in the ... discipline prescribed by Congress; the ... by the Consent of the particular States, and the ... purchased by the Consent of the Legisla- ... — And ... his Constitution

All Pet... ...this Constitution, or which shall be made, under the Authority ... Constitution or Laws of ... ... of the United Stat... required as a Qualificat...

We the People

of the United States, in order to for ... insure domestic Tranquility, provide for the common defence, promote the general Welfare, and se ... and our Posterity, do ordain and establish this Constitution for the United States of America.

Article. I.

Section. 1. All legislative Powers herein granted shall be vested in a Congress of the United Stat ... Representatives.

Section. 2. The House of Representatives shall be composed of Members chosen every second Yea ... each State shall have the Qualifications requisite for Electors of the most numerous Branch of the State Leg ...

No Person shall be a Representative who shall not have attained to the Age of twenty five Yea ... d who shall not, when elected, be an Inhabitant of that State in which he shall be chosen.

Representatives and direct Taxes shall be apportioned among the several States which may be inc ... mber, which shall be determined by adding to the whole Number of free Persons, including those bou ... taxed, three fifths of all other Persons. The actual Enumeration shall be made within three Year ... within every subsequent Term of ten Years, in such Manner as they shall by Law direct. The N ... Thousand, but each State shall have at Least one Representative; and until such enumeratio ... d to chuse three; Massachusetts eight; Rhode Island and Providence Plantations one; Conn ... Delaware one; Maryland six; Virginia ten; North Carolina five; South Carolina f ... When vacancies happen in the Representation from any State, the Executive Autho ... ... the Representation from any State, the ... and shall have

James Madison Today

Madison died at the age of 85. A building was made to honor Madison in Washington, D.C., in 1976. The building has a large library to honor Madison. Madison Square Garden in New York City is also named for him. People go there to see sports events and hear music groups.

MADISON SQUARE GARDEN

21

JAMES MADISON FACTS

These pages provide detailed information that expands on the interesting facts found in the book. These pages are intended to be used by adults to help young readers round out their knowledge of each historical figure featured in the *Founding Fathers* series.

Pages 4–5

Who Is James Madison? James Madison is known as the "Father of the Constitution" because he wrote many parts of that historic document. At 29 years old, Madison was the youngest member of the Continental Congress, a group of colonial delegates who created the new American government. Of the 39 men who signed the Constitution, only Madison and George Washington later became president of the United States.

Pages 6–7

What Is a Founding Father? The Founding Fathers of the United States of America played a significant role in forming the country. Though there are no specific requirements for inclusion in this elite group, a Founding Father is typically a person who was involved in, or contributed to, one of the founding events of the United States. These events include the American Revolution, the creation and signing of the Declaration of Independence, and the Constitutional Convention, in which the Constitution of the United States of America was written.

Pages 8–9

Growing Up Nicknamed "Jemmy," James Madison was born at Montpelier, his grandparents' Virginia plantation. He lived there most of his life. Madison completed much of his schooling at home with the help of a private tutor his father hired. He also attended boarding school for five years as a teenager. Although a shy and sickly youth, Madison had a sharp mind and went on to receive a classical education at the College of New Jersey, now Princeton University.

Pages 10–11

Learning From Others Madison's first great influence was his early teacher, Donald Robertson, whom Madison met when he was 12 years old. About Robertson, Madison said, "All that I have been in life I owe largely to that man." As an adult, Madison was Thomas Jefferson's advisor, secretary of state, and lifelong friend. Together, they created the University of Virginia in 1825.

Practice Makes Perfect Madison joined the Virginia militia as a colonel, but poor health kept him from serving. From his studies, he gained a deep understanding of history, foreign countries, and hundreds of political systems. Madison was elected to the Virginia Legislature at age 25 and helped write its state constitution. He wrote speeches to clarify his ideas and honed his political skills in Congress. He served four terms in Congress..

Key Events At just 36 years old, Madison became the primary author of the Bill of Rights. He envisioned a balanced government, one that would protect its citizens but not so powerful that essential freedoms would be lost. Among the bill's 10 amendments, Madison included the right to freedom of speech, the right to a public trial, and protection from unreasonable search and seizure.

Challenges Though Madison encountered many difficulties during his presidency, none were as challenging as The War of 1812. Among many bitter conflicts, the British captured American trade ships and took over coastal cities. The Americans burned the city of York, now Toronto, Canada. On August 24, 1814, the British attacked and burned Washington, D.C. Luckily, Madison and his wife escaped unharmed.

A Nation Is Born Twenty-two years after signing the U.S. Constitution, James Madison was elected president. He was a popular choice and received about 70 percent of the electoral votes. Madison was a champion of the people's rights and focused especially on religious freedom. He served two terms as president, from 1809 to 1817.

James Madison Today Madison died at Montpelier on June 28, 1836. The Madison Memorial Building, the official memorial to James Madison, houses part of the Library of Congress. It, the Pentagon, and the FBI building are the three largest public buildings in the Washington, D.C. area. Madison Square Garden first opened in New York City in 1879. It has been rebuilt several times since then. "The Garden" hosts many special events and is home to the oldest National Hockey League arena.

KEY WORDS

Research has shown that as much as 65 percent of all written material published in English is made up of 300 words. These 300 words cannot be taught using pictures or learned by sounding them out. They must be recognized by sight. This book contains 87 common sight words to help young readers improve their reading fluency and comprehension. This book also teaches young readers several important content words, such as nouns. These words are paired with pictures to aid in learning and improve understanding.

Page	Sight Words First Appearance
4	a, and, as, because, for, from, he, his, is, of, one, the, this, to, used, was
7	American, are, be, country, how, new, people, says, these
8	an, at, father, home, important, in, liked, most, often, on, read, took, when, young
10	about, books, day, great, had, him, ideas, many, named, soon, well
13	began, different, enough, found, go, have, help, later, not, out, way, would
14	after, by, live, other, should, talk, their, went, with, years
17	group, hands, into, or, work
18	keep, make, rights, that
20	also, has, hear, large, see, there

Page	Content Words First Appearance
4	America, Founding Fathers, freedom, James Madison, laws, president skills, thinker, United States, writer
7	colonies, form, Great Britain, rule, United States of America, U.S. Constitution
8	March, inside, landowner, Port Conway, schooling, Virginia
10	teacher
13	army, government, law, Virginia, war
14	rules
17	person, power
20	age, building, events, library, Madison Square Garden, New York City, sports, Washington, D.C.